HOMEMADE TREE TRIMMINGS

Decorating the Christmas tree is a tradition that is also a favorite family pastime, with ornaments used year after year becoming treasured possessions. And it is often the homemade ornaments that become the favorites, for something of the maker goes into the craft. The beauty that delights the eye also warms the heart with memories that will long be cherished.

Featured in this book are a variety of ornaments you can make yourself. From fabric to paper, yarn to straw, yucca pods to clothespins, there is something for everyone to try. Some projects require considerable patience and skill; others are less demanding and can be done by children. All will add a special touch to the tree. What's more, these lovely pieces make wonderful gifts for friends. And they're popular sellers at holiday bazaars and gift fairs.

When trimming the tree, don't forget to include some special one-season touches, too. Prepare your favorite sugar cookie dough, cut it into Christmas shapes and make a small hole in the top of each cookie before baking. Once baked, decorate the cookie with sparkling candies and run a thread through the hole for hanging. (Be sure to keep plenty of fresh cookies on hand to fill in the bare spots as these ornaments disappear from the tree!)

You can also add fragrances to your tree by making clusters of spices and tying them to the branches with thread or fine wire. Use stick cinnamon, coriander, juniper berries, caraway seeds, coffee beans, cardamom, gingerroot, allspice, cloves, fennel or whatever else strikes your fancy. The spicy scents will last long after the holidays are over.

As a final touch, tie plaid and solid-colored bows to the branches, or string popcorn, cranberries, Indian corn and small pinecones and loop them around your tree. Make shiny foil paper chains, or drape the needles with glistening tinsel.

And when you're finished, turn on the Christmas music, serve some Christmas punch and sit before your tree to enjoy the warm glow that fills your home.

WREATH ORNAMENT

These lovely traditional ornaments are easy to make and take only a bit of time. Try making them in different sizes. They're great for trimming a package . . . or hanging on the door of a dollhouse!

You will need:

2 strips of fabric, 16½" x 2½"
needle and thread
polyester fiberfill

42" length of red cording
16" length of ½" velvet ribbon
string or fishing line

Instructions:

1. Turn under the ends of the fabric strips ¼" and stitch.
2. Place the right sides of the fabric strips together. Stitch ¼" seams up both sides, leaving the ends open. This will form a tube.
3. Turn the fabric tube right-side out and stuff with fiberfill.
4. Bring the ends of the tube together to form a wreath shape. Stitch the ends together.
5. Wrap the red cording around the wreath, tightening as desired to form puffiness. (See Diagram 1.) Stitch the ends of the cording to the wreath at the point where the ends of the wreath tube come together.
6. Tie a bow with the velvet ribbon around the wreath to hide the ends of the cording.
7. Tie a string or stitch a length of fishing line through the top of the wreath, tying a loop for hanging.

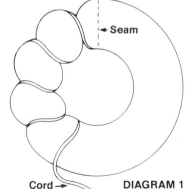

Seam

Cord → DIAGRAM 1

TOY DRUM

The rum-a-tum-tum of a little toy drum brings all kinds of Christmas memories to mind. Here's a simple and clever way to make a colorful toy for your tree.

You will need:

toilet paper or paper towel tube
heavy white paper or poster board
pencil
scissors
liquid white glue
2½" wide red velveteen ribbon
20" length of gold cord

straight pins
7" length of gold braid
gold doily
seed pearls
small round stick, such as a cotton
　swab, painted red
gold thread

Instructions:

1. Cut a length of tubing, 2½" long. Place the end of the tube on heavy paper or poster board and draw around it to make two circles. Cut out the circles and glue them to the top and bottom of the cut tube.
2. Cut the red velveteen ribbon to wrap around the tube and glue in place.
3. Start at the seam of the velveteen ribbon and zigzag gold cord from top to bottom all the way around the drum, holding the cord in place with straight pins. When the cord is arranged to your satisfaction, glue in place as shown in Diagram 1. Remove or leave in pins, as desired.
4. Cut and glue the gold braid around the top and bottom of the drum.
5. Cut small circular pieces from the doily. Stick a pin through a seed pearl, and then through a doily circle and into a section along the side of the drum. Repeat for each section.
6. Break the small stick in half and glue both halves to the top of the drum as drumsticks.
7. Tie gold thread through a loop of braid at the top of the drum for hanging.

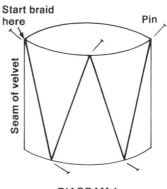

DIAGRAM 1

3

CANDY CANE ORNAMENT

Here's a cute and clever way to put some yummy-looking candy canes on your tree . . . and these won't be taken down and eaten, either!

You will need:

tracing paper
pencil
scissors
9" square fabric remnant for each
   cane

needle and thread
polyester fiberfill
50" length of ⅜" velvet ribbon
liquid white glue
string or fishing line

Instructions:

1. Lay a piece of tracing paper over the cane pattern; trace around the pattern and cut it out.
2. Lay the pattern on a double thickness of fabric (fold your fabric square in half) and cut out. You will have two pieces.
3. Place the right sides of the two pieces of fabric together. Stitch all the way around the cane, leaving a 1" opening on the inside "stem" of the cane.
4. Carefully clip around curves to keep from puckering.
5. Turn the cane right-side out and stuff with fiberfill. Stitch the opening shut.
6. Cut a 32" length from the ribbon. Trim one end to meet the point of the candy cane. (See Diagram 1.) Glue the ribbon in place. Wrap the ribbon around the candy cane; trim off any overlap at the end and glue in place.
7. With the remaining 18" length of ribbon, tie a bow at the arch of the cane.
8. Tie string or a length of fishing line around the ribbon at the top of the cane, making a loop for hanging.

DIAGRAM 1

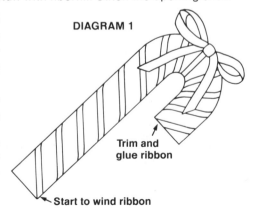

Trim and glue ribbon

Start to wind ribbon

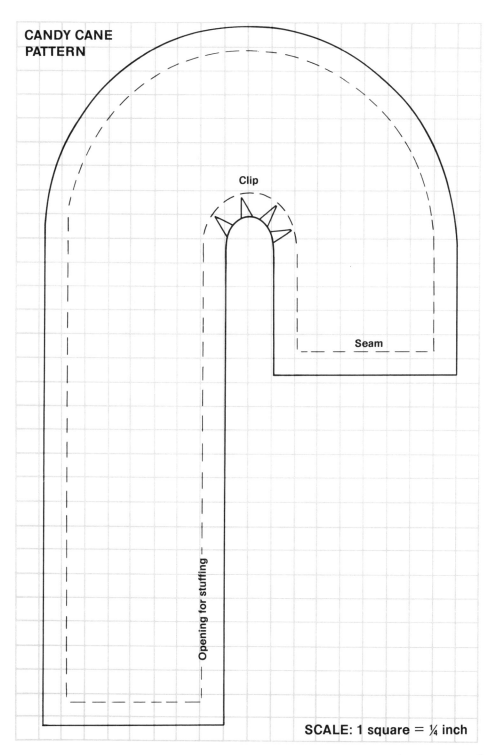

CANDY CANE
PATTERN

Clip

Seam

Opening for stuffing

SCALE: 1 square = ¼ inch

5

PEEK-A-BOO STOCKING

Who's the cutie peeking out of this stocking? A little Christmas mouse to add a delightful touch to your tree! We've included the pattern for the mouse here . . . but you can make kittens, puppies, elves or other folk to peep out from the little pocket.

You will need:

tracing paper
pencil
scissors
7" x 10" fabric remnant
scraps of felt in gray, pink, brown and
    white

assorted rickrack, ribbon, pompons
    and a bell
liquid white glue
polyester fiberfill
needle and thread
brown embroidery floss

Instructions:

1. Lay tracing paper on the stocking pattern. Trace and cut out.
2. Place the pattern on a double thickness of fabric (fold the remnant in half) and cut out the stocking form. You will have two pieces.
3. Decorate the right side of one of the stocking pieces as shown in the photo. Using the patterns, cut out the heel, toe and pocket from white felt and glue in place. Trim with white rickrack glued in place.
4. At the top of each stocking piece, turn under ¼" and stitch.
5. Place the stocking pieces right sides together and stitch a ¼" seam all the way around *except* for the top, which should be left open.
6. Turn the stocking right-side out. Stuff with fiberfill and sew the top opening shut. Glue a piece of rickrack all the way across the top.
7. Lay tracing paper over the mouse patterns. Trace and cut out. Lay the patterns on pieces of felt and cut out.
8. Glue the pieces in place on the stocking as shown here. Use brown floss to stitch in the mouse's whiskers, using the outline stitch shown in the Stitchery Glossary on the inside back cover. Add a small bow just below the ear if desired. Sew a pompon or bell to the toe of the stocking.
9. Add a loop for hanging.

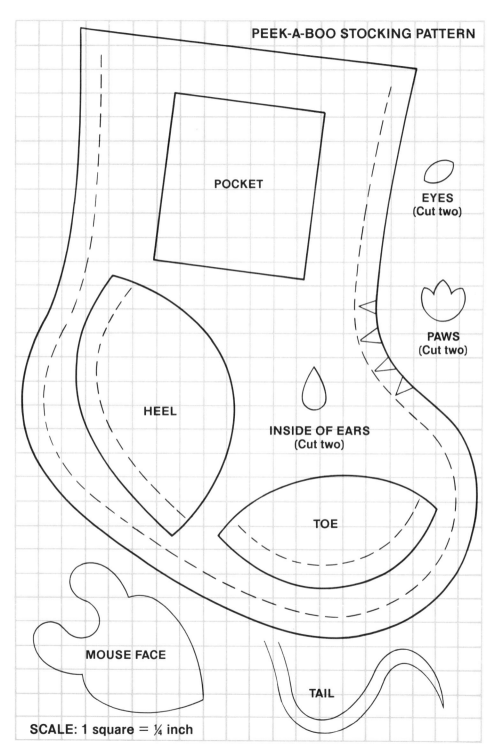

PEEK-A-BOO STOCKING PATTERN

POCKET

EYES
(Cut two)

PAWS
(Cut two)

HEEL

INSIDE OF EARS
(Cut two)

TOE

MOUSE FACE

TAIL

SCALE: 1 square = ¼ inch

7

VELVET STRAWBERRY

What could be yummier than a velvet strawberry hanging among the evergreen branches of your Christmas tree? Just a scrap of fabric and felt, some stuffing and some stitches and you have it made!

You will need:

tracing paper	seed pearls
pencil	polyester fiberfill
scissors	green felt
6'' square piece of red velvet	liquid white glue
needle and thread	

Instructions:

1. Lay a piece of tracing paper on the patterns provided and trace. Cut out the paper patterns. Lay the strawberry pattern on the red velvet and cut out.
2. Fold the strawberry piece, plush side inside, so that sides A and B meet; sew a ¼'' seam. Turn the strawberry right-side out. Run a long gathering stitch around the border of the top edge, but don't pull it tight yet!
3. Sew on seed pearls as shown on the pattern and knot on the wrong side of the fabric.
4. Stuff the strawberry with fiberfill.
5. Cut the stem and strawberry leaves from green felt. Loop the stem in half and stick the ends of the stem into the fiberfill at the top of the strawberry. Pull the gathering thread and sew the top of the strawberry shut, sewing the stem in place at the same time.
6. Slip the strawberry leaves over the stem and glue in place.
7. Attach a thread loop to the stem to hang.

VELVET STRAWBERRY PATTERN

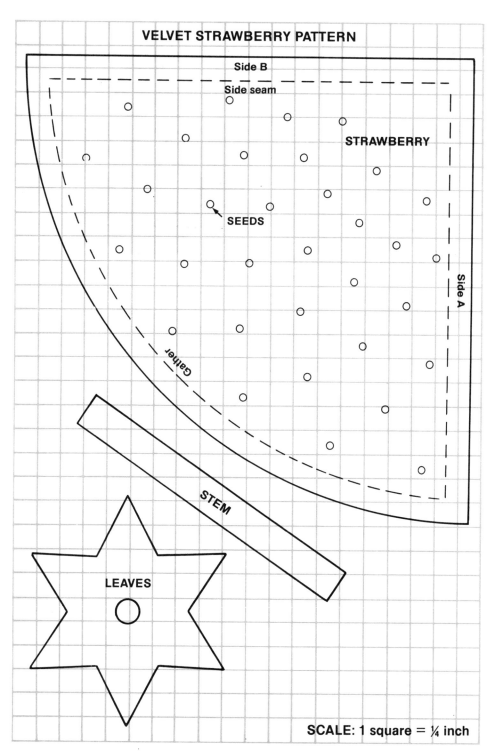

Side B

Side seam

STRAWBERRY

Side A

SEEDS

Gather

STEM

LEAVES

SCALE: 1 square = ¼ inch

POMPON SANTA

Ho ho ho! Everyone looks for Santa at Christmas time. Here's a simple way to craft this jolly fellow to hang from your tree.

You will need:

liquid white glue
1 white pompon—golf ball size*
1 red pompon—slightly larger than the white*
4 small red pompons—gumball size*

red, yellow and black felt
red and white sport yarn
size B crochet hook
needle and thread

Instructions:

1. Glue the white pompon to the largest red pompon to form Santa's body and head.
2. Glue two of the smaller red pompons together to form each arm, then glue them to Santa's body.
3. Cut two small black felt circles, one small red felt circle, and two small yellow felt circles. Glue the black circles to Santa's face to make eyes, the red circle to Santa's face for a nose. Glue the yellow circles down the front of Santa's body to make buttons.
4. To make Santa's mustache, cut several pieces of white sport yarn 1½" long. Tie them together in the center and fluff out. Glue under Santa's nose.
5. Santa's hat is crocheted. To make the hat, use the red yarn. Chain 4 and join in a circle. (See Diagrams 1-3, page 12.)
   Row 1: ch 2, 9 dc in circle
   Row 2: ch 2, (1 dc in first dc, 2 dc in next dc), repeat for total of 16 dc
   Row 3: ch 2, (1 dc in first dc, 2 dc in next dc), repeat for total of 24 dc
   Row 4: ch 2, (1 dc in first 3 dc, 2 dc in next dc), repeat for a total of 30 dc
   Row 5-8: repeat row 4, end off
   Row 9: join on white sport yarn and sc in each dc, end off
   Glue on the hat; allow to dry. Chain a string of red yarn for the loop at the top of the hat; sew on for hanger.

*You may wish to make your own pompons by wrapping several rounds of yarn around a piece of cardboard that is half the desired width of the pompon. Cut the yarn off the cardboard and tightly tie in the center with a piece of yarn. Fan out the yarn to make the pompon. Trim the uneven end. (See Diagram 4.)

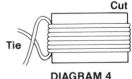

DIAGRAM 4

SNOWMAN ORNAMENT

Here's a "jolly, happy soul" who won't melt away like Frosty . . . he'll be around for years to add a bright touch to your tree.

You will need:

sport yarn in white, red, green and gray
size D crochet hook

cotton stuffing
felt scraps in black and orange
black embroidery thread
needle and white thread

Instructions:
Gauge 7 sc = 1" (See crochet diagrams on page 12.)

Head and Body:
Begin at top of head with white, ch 2
Rnd 1: 6 sc in 2nd ch
Rnd 2: 2 sc in each sc
Rnd 3: (sc in next sc, 2 sc in next sc), repeat 6 times + 18 sc
Rnd 4: (sc in each of next 2 sc, 2 sc in next sc), repeat 6 times = 24 sc
Rnds 5-8: work even for 4 rnds
Rnd 9: (sc in each of next 2 sc, work next 2 sc together), repeat 6 times = 18 sc
Rnd 10: (sc in next sc, work next 2 sc together), repeat 6 times = 12 sc
Rnd 11: work even
Rnd 12 and 13: repeat 3 and 4 - 24 sc
Rnd 14-19: work even for 6 rnds
Rnd 20: repeat 9
Rnd 21: work even, end off

Leg (make two) ch 7
Rnd 1: sc in 2nd sc from hook
sc in next 4 ch, 5 sc in end ch
sc in next 4 ch on opposite side
2 sc in last sc
Rnd 2 and 3: work even 16 sc
Rnd 4: sc in each of 6 sc (work next 2 sc together), twice sc in each of 6 sc
Rnd 5-9: work even 5 rnds 14 sc, end off

Arm (make two) ch 2
Rnd 1: 6 sc in 2nd ch from hook
Rnd 2: 2 sc in each sc
Rbd 3-9: work even on 12 sc for 7 rnds, end off

Scarf: starting with red ch 5
Rnd 1: sc in 2nd ch from hook; sc in next 3 ch - 4 sc, turn
Rnd 2: ch 1 sc in next 4 sc, turn; drop red, do not cut
Rnd 3: pick up green, ch 1, sc in next 4 sc, turn
Rnd 4: ch 1, sc in next 4 sc, turn
Rnd 5: bring red up, ch 1, sc in next 4 sc, turn
Rnd 6: repeat 2

11

Continue alternating red and green until scarf is 10" long—end with red.
Fringe: cut two 2" lengths of green yarn—slip stitch through each of 4 sc in both ends; trim evenly.

Hat: with gray ch 6, slip stitch in first ch to form ring
    Rnd 1: 2 sc in each ch - 12 sc
    Rnd 2: work even
    Rnd 3: 2 sc in each sc - 24 sc
    Rnd 4: sc in *inside* loop only of each sc - 24 sc
    Rnd 5-9: work even
    Rnd 10: 2 sc in *outside* loop only of each sc - 48 sc; end off

Finishing:

1. Stuff body, arms and legs; sew up openings.
2. Sew arms and legs to body. Sew on hat, leaving edge to form a brim.
3. Make face by gluing on two black felt dots for eyes; fold over a triangle of orange felt and glue in place for a carrot nose. Embroider mouth using chain stitch in black. (See Stitchery Glossary, inside back cover.)
4. Tie scarf around neck.
5. Chain a strand of embroidery thread for hanging loop and sew to top of hat.

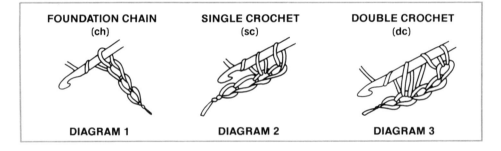

FOUNDATION CHAIN
(ch)

SINGLE CROCHET
(sc)

DOUBLE CROCHET
(dc)

DIAGRAM 1　　　　**DIAGRAM 2**　　　　**DIAGRAM 3**

CAT ANGEL

Here's a sweet kitty with an extra special surprise inside. She's a little sack that will keep some goodie or tiny gift hidden. Undo the ribbon at the top and she opens up . . . just the thing to hang on the tree or stuff into a stocking!

You will need:

7½" length of 1" wide white lace
7½" x 5" fabric remnant
14" thin green ribbon
small safety pin
tracing paper and pencil
scraps of felt in dark pink, light pink, white and black

pink embroidery floss
needle and thread
liquid white glue
gold braid
cotton

Instructions:

1. Sew the lace to the bottom (7½" edge) of the fabric, without going over the edge.
2. Form a casing along the top 7½" edge by turning under twice and stitching ¼" from the edge. Leave a small opening somewhere in the back.
3. Fold the fabric, right sides together, and sew a ¼" seam along the bottom and side. Turn right-side out. Fasten the small safety pin to the ribbon and thread the ribbon through the casing, using the safety pin as a guide.
4. Lay tracing paper over the patterns for the wings, feet, paws and facial features. Trace and cut out the patterns. Lay the patterns on the felt and cut out using the white for the wings and outer ears; pink for cheeks, paws and feet; dark pink for nose, inner ears and paw pads; black for eyes.
5. Blanket stitch around the wings. (See Stitchery Glossary, inside back cover.) Glue the inner ears to the outer ears and the paw pads to the paws.
6. Glue the wings, paws, feet, eyes, nose and cheeks in place as shown in the photo.
7. Embroider the mouth, using the chain stitch. (See Stitchery Glossary, inside back cover.)
8. Sew a gold braid halo in place, securing it at the back where the ribbon is tied.
9. Stuff the bag with cotton, then add candy, a small gift or a sachet if you wish.

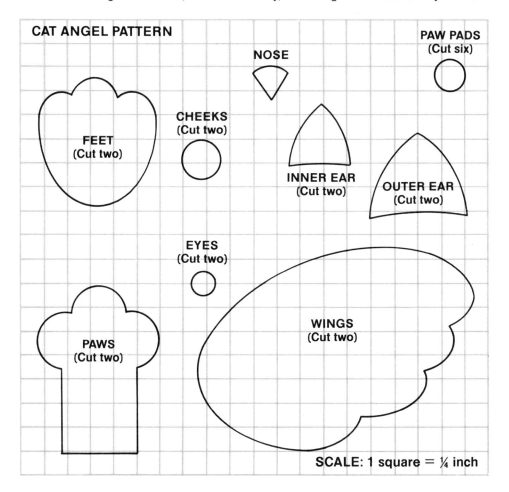

CAT ANGEL PATTERN

NOSE

PAW PADS
(Cut six)

CHEEKS
(Cut two)

FEET
(Cut two)

INNER EAR
(Cut two)

OUTER EAR
(Cut two)

EYES
(Cut two)

WINGS
(Cut two)

PAWS
(Cut two)

SCALE: 1 square = ¼ inch

YUCCA POD CLOWN

In the Southwest, yucca pods are abundant in the early fall and throughout the winter months. Here's how to turn your pods into clever little clowns to brighten your Christmas tree.

You will need:

a yucca pod with stem removed
an acorn (with "hat" removed) or other round nut
poster paints and paintbrush
fabric and felt scraps

orange yarn
2 pompons
scissors
liquid white glue
gold thread or string

Instructions:

1. Paint the "prongs" of the pod white; paint the tips black.
2. Cut fabric scraps to cover the outside part of the prongs; glue in place as shown in photo.
3. Cut arms and a pointed or scalloped collar from white felt and glue in place as shown in Diagrams 1 and 2.
4. Paint the acorn or nut pink; when dry, paint on eyes, nose and mouth. Glue the nut onto the stem end of the yucca pod after removing the stem (on top of the collar). (See Diagram 1.)
5. Glue a star and pompons to the collar. Glue yarn in place for hair. Form a cone from felt for the hat and glue in place. Glue a star to the hat. (See Diagram 2.)
6. Tie gold thread or string firmly below the rim of the hat and loop for hanging.

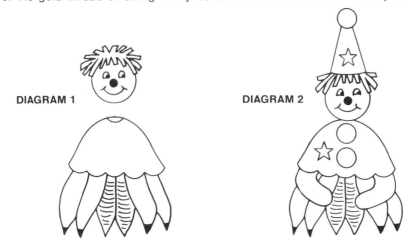

DIAGRAM 1

DIAGRAM 2

BABY'S FIRST CHRISTMAS ORNAMENT

This wonderful ornament will quickly become a tradition to be passed on from generation to generation. Give one as a gift to friends who have just had a baby . . . and if it's a new idea, remember the older children, too. They'll also want to be featured on their Christmas tree!

You will need:

tracing paper
pencil
scissors
2 pieces of 9" square calico plus 1
   smaller square of calico or a
   complimentary-colored fabric
polyester fiberfill
needle and thread
square mat with an inner pre-cut
   circle (See Step 5.)

small photo of child
manicure scissors
double-sided tape
liquid white glue
trim or braid
thin cardboard or heavy paper
felt scrap
fabric glue

Instructions:

1. Lay a piece of tracing paper over the star pattern. Trace and cut out.
2. Lay the pattern on the squares of calico fabric, right sides together, and cut out.
3. With the right sides still together, stitch a ¼" seam around the star, leaving a 1½" opening. (See Pattern 1, page 17.)
4. Clip the corners to prevent puckering. Turn the star right-side out and stuff with fiberfill. Stitch the opening closed.
5. Cut or buy a pre-cut circle inside a square mat that will fit inside the star shape without overlapping the edges. (See Pattern 2, page 16.) The circle should be the right size to frame the photo.
6. Cut a square of fabric ½" larger than the mat all the way around. Lay the mat on the top of the wrong side of the fabric, making sure the mat is centered. Use a pencil to draw the outline of the circle on the fabric.
7. Use the manicure scissors to cut a circle in the fabric slightly smaller than the circle you have drawn. Clip around the circle as shown in Pattern 3, page 16.
8. Place double-sided tape on the mat and stick tufts of fiberfill to the tape at even intervals.
9. Put the fabric with the cut-out circle over the tufted side of the mat. Stretch the outside ends and the middle of the circle edges over the fiberfill to the back side of the mat and staple or secure with glue. It's like stretching a canvas to make a stuffed frame . . . a bit tricky but it doesn't have to be perfect.
10. Glue around the inside of the circle edge to cover any rough borders.

11. Place the stuffed mat over a piece of thin cardboard or heavy paper cut slightly smaller than the mat size. Use a pencil to draw the outline of the circle on the paper.
12. Using the pencil outline as a guide, glue the photo to this paper. Glue the edges of the paper to the stuffed fabric mat so the photo shows through the circle.
13. Glue a square of felt to the back of the stuffed mat and photo. When dry, glue this piece to the star pillow using fabric glue.
14. Sew a trim hanger to the top of the star.

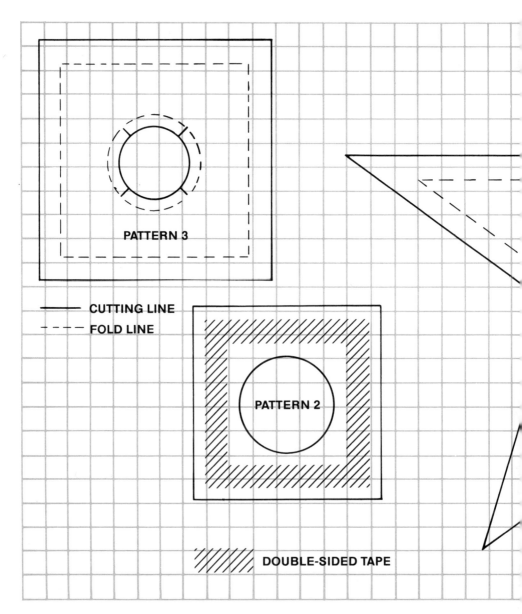

PATTERN 3

CUTTING LINE
FOLD LINE

PATTERN 2

DOUBLE-SIDED TAPE

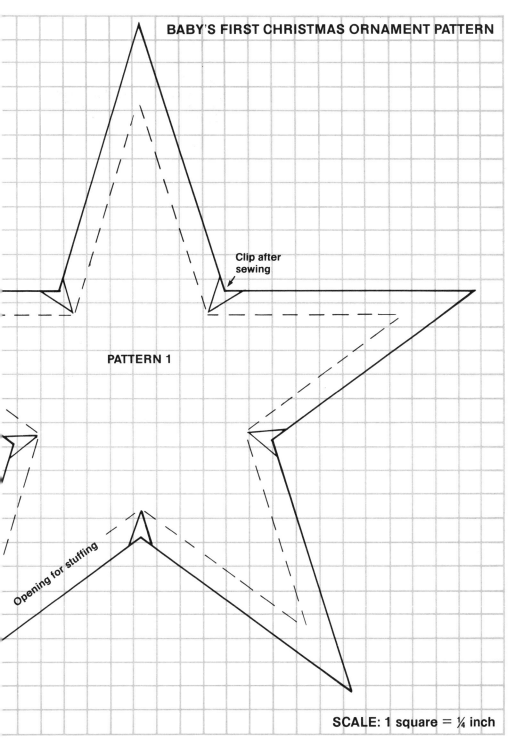

BABY'S FIRST CHRISTMAS ORNAMENT PATTERN

Clip after sewing

PATTERN 1

Opening for stuffing

SCALE: 1 square = ¼ inch

17

GINGERBREAD PEOPLE

These delightful little ornaments are such fun to make! You might even want to invite some children to help you with the stuffing and trimming.

You will need:

tracing paper
¼ yard fabric or a 9" x 12" remnant for each ornament
2 buttons for the eyes
crewel yarn or embroidery floss for the mouth
1 yard rickrack
a needle and thread
liquid white glue
assorted yarn, ribbon, lace; scraps of felt and fabric
polyester fiberfill

Instructions:

1. Lay a piece of tracing paper over the body pattern; trace and cut out.
2. Lay the pattern on a double thickness of fabric and cut out. You will have two pieces.
3. On the piece you are going to use for the front, sew on the button eyes. See X's on pattern for placement.
4. With embroidery floss or crewel yarn, embroider on the mouth using the outline stitch. (See Stitchery Glossary, inside back cover.)
5. Place the right sides of the two pieces face to face and stitch together using a ¼" seam and leaving a 2" opening on the inside of one of the legs.
6. Carefully clip all the way around the seam to keep the curves from puckering, then turn right-side out.
7. Stuff with polyester fiberfill; stitch the opening closed.
8. Sew or glue rickrack all the way around the gingerbread ornament, covering the seam as you go. You are now ready to decorate!

Decorating Ideas:

1. Cut circle or heart shapes from felt to make cheeks and glue onto the face with liquid white glue.
2. Tie a yarn or ribbon bow around its neck.
3. Glue or sew pieces of lace or appliqué to the fronts to make bibs, collars, etc. Embellish with tiny beads, pearls and buttons. Glue bits of lace to the hands and feet.
4. Paint with acrylics.
5. Sew a vest for your ornament! Lay tracing paper over the pattern provided; trace and cut out. You may want to reinforce your fabric first so you won't have to turn under the edges. To do this, iron fusible interfacing to the back of your fabric before cutting. Lay patterns on fabric and cut one back, one left side front, and one right side front. Lay right sides of the front pieces on the back and stitch ¼" seams at the shoulders and sides. Turn right-side out. You may need to adjust the seams to fit your ornament just right.
6. Tack a ribbon or rickrack loop to the back of the head and hang as a tree ornament.
7. Tack several gingerbread people together and string on the tree, across the mantel, or anywhere you like! Have fun!

GINGERBREAD PEOPLE PATTERN

CUTTING LINE ——————
STITCHING LINE — —

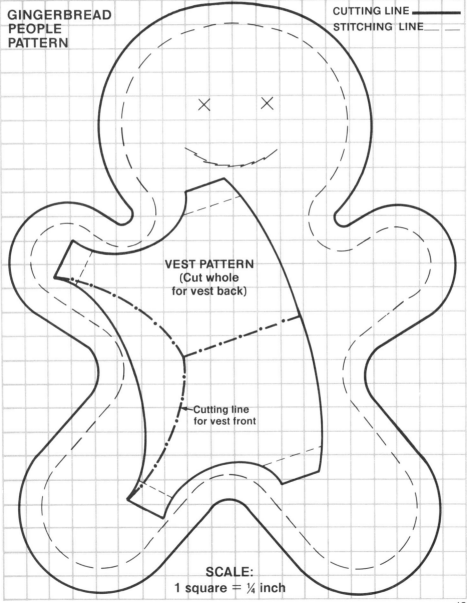

VEST PATTERN
(Cut whole
for vest back)

Cutting line
for vest front

SCALE:
1 square = ¼ inch

BABY STOCKING ANGEL

You will need:

white cotton newborn-size baby sock with decorative cuff
scissors
polyester fiberfill
2 blue seed beads or blue embroidery floss
needle and white thread
10" lacy pleated trim, 4" wide (pre-gathered optional)
8" each of two colors of ⅛" wide ribbon
5 or 6 pearl stamens
velour leaf
rouge or blush-on

Instructions:

1. Gather the sock 1" from the top (or just under the decorative cuff). Draw the thread tight and fold down the cuff, leaving enough thread for a hanging loop. The cuff forms a halo. (See Diagram 1.)
2. Cut off the toe of the sock and stuff the sock with fiberfill. (See Diagram 1.)
3. Baste around the bottom of the ribbing with long stitches. Pull the thread taut and tie a knot at the back of the head to form the neck.
4. Insert a needle from the back of the neck to the front of the head and sew on the seed beads for eyes. (See Diagram 2.) Or, if you prefer, embroider some eyes with blue embroidery floss.
5. Stuff more fiberfill into the bottom half of the sock. The sock heel will be the hands. Push the fiberfill into the chest area and make an indentation under the chest and above the hands. (See Diagram 3.)
6. Making all knots in the back of the neck, insert the needle and bring it out under the chest. Make two big stitches up and down (one on top of the other) to make the hands, pulling the thread tight. (See Diagram 3.) Bring the needle out through the back of the neck and tie a knot.
7. Add more fiberfill and pinch up some of the stuffed sock to form the angel's behind. Insert the needle in the back of the neck and bring out in the middle of the angel's behind. Make one big stitch down the center to form a crease and pull tight. Bring the needle out the front, under the tummy, and make long stitches down to the toes to form the angel's legs. (See Diagrams 4 and 5.) Stitch the opening closed.
8. To make the wings, cut the lacy pleated trim in half and gather each piece into a fan shape. Sew the pieces together to form butterfly wings. (See Diagram 6.) Sew the wings to the angel's back.
9. Tie a bow around the angel's neck with both narrow ribbons, trimming the ends. Tack a little bouquet of pearl stamens and a velour leaf in the indentation above the angel's hands.
10. Put rouge or blush-on on the angel's face and behind. Now your soft sculpture angel is ready to hang on your tree!

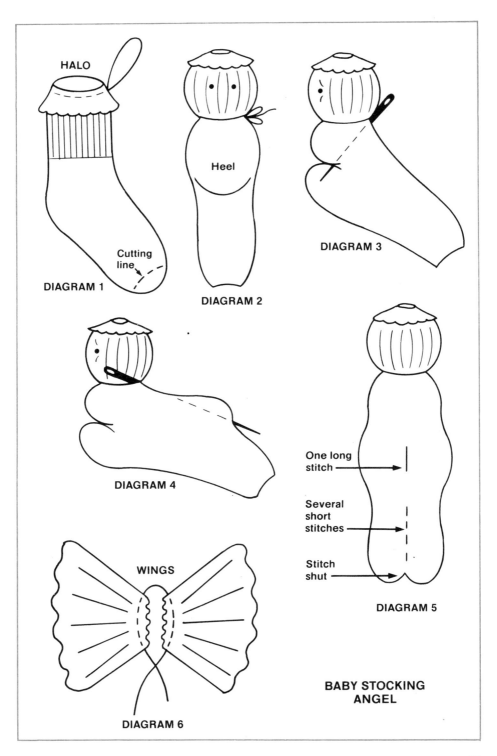

HALO

Cutting line

DIAGRAM 1

Heel

DIAGRAM 2

DIAGRAM 3

DIAGRAM 4

One long stitch

Several short stitches

Stitch shut

DIAGRAM 5

WINGS

DIAGRAM 6

BABY STOCKING ANGEL

CLOTHESPIN CAROLERS

These two unique songsters make a wonderful addition to the tree . . . and both start with simple, old-fashioned clothespins. This handsome young couple would also be right at home in a shadowbox or a little girl's stocking.

CAROLING WOMAN

You will need:

old-fashioned wooden clothespin
tracing paper
pencil
scissors
scraps of fabric, felt and lace
needle and thread
floral wire

embroidery floss
liquid white glue
tweezers
manicure scissors
small pearl beads
scrap of heavy paper
black and pink felt-tip markers

Instructions:

1. Lay the tracing paper over the bodice pattern on page 24. Trace and cut out. Lay the pattern over the fabric; cut out. Cut out another rectangle that measures 3½" x 9" from the fabric; this will be the skirt.
2. Hem the top and bottom of the skirt. Sew lace trim to the bottom. Sew a seam up the back. Run a gathering stitch around the top. Sew under the arm and side seams of the bodice.
3. Wrap wire around the head of the clothespin and extend on both sides for arms as shown in Diagram 1 for the Caroling Man. (See page 23.) Glue the bodice in place, turning under the raw edge in back. Cut out hands from pink felt and glue to the ends of the wire. Glue pieces of lace for cuffs over the raw edges of the sleeves. Glue pearls at the neck front to cover the raw edge.
4. Gather the skirt at the waist; stitch in place on doll.
5. Tie several strands of 4" long embroidery floss in the center; glue in place for hair. Cut the bonnet (see pattern, page 24) from a piece of felt and glue to the head. Stitch thread through the top of the bonnet and tie in a loop for hanging.
6. Make the felt music book by cutting a rectangle of felt 1" x ⅝" and gluing a smaller rectangle of heavy paper inside. Fold in the middle. Bend the arms and glue the book to the hands.
7. Draw in eyes, mouth and pink cheeks with felt-tip markers.

CAROLING MAN

You will need:

acrylic paints and paintbrush
old-fashioned wooden clothespin
florist wire
black embroidery floss
liquid white glue
black felt-tip marker
felt scraps in gray, dark green, black
  and pink

needle and thread
tracing paper
pencil
scissors
fabric scraps
scrap of heavy paper
lace trim
tweezers

Instructions:

1. Paint the clothespin prongs gray for the trousers. Paint a black stripe down the sides and on the very tips for shoes.
2. Wrap wire around the head and extend on both sides for arms. (See Diagram 1.)
3. Loop the embroidery floss for hair and glue it to the top of the clothespin. Shape it neatly around the head to the back.
4. Use the felt-tip marker to draw on bangs, sideburns, eyes and a mustache.
5. Trace the hat patterns (A and B) on page 24. Lay the patterns on the gray felt and cut out. Glue the edges of the strip to form a cylinder. Glue the cylinder to the base of the hat. Cut a small black strip for the hat band and glue it around. Glue the hat to the top of the head and sew thread or cord through the top of the hat, making a loop for hanging.
6. Lay tracing paper over the jacket pattern as shown on page 24. Trace and cut out. Lay the pattern over a piece of fabric (black or green felt would look great!) and cut on solid line.
7. With the right sides of the fabric together, sew a ¼" seam on the undersleeve and along the side. Turn right-side out and fit over the doll, carefully extending the wire through the sleeves. Trim the front and back tails as indicated by lines on pattern.
8. Cut two hands from pink felt and glue them to the wire. Glue lace trim cuffs around the sleeves. Use tweezers to help put the pieces in place if you need to.
9. Make the felt music book by cutting a rectangle of felt 1" x ⅝" and gluing a smaller rectangle of heavy paper inside. Fold the book in half, bend the arms and glue the hands to the book.
10. For the scarf, cut a strip of colorful fabric ½" x 7". Press the edges under and fray the ends. Wrap the scarf around the doll's neck and tie in place.
11. If you like, tuck small pieces of white paper into the coat to look like a collar. Take a look at your man . . . you might have to glue here and there to make everything look just right!

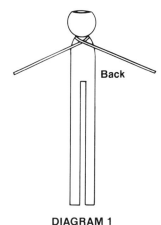

DIAGRAM 1

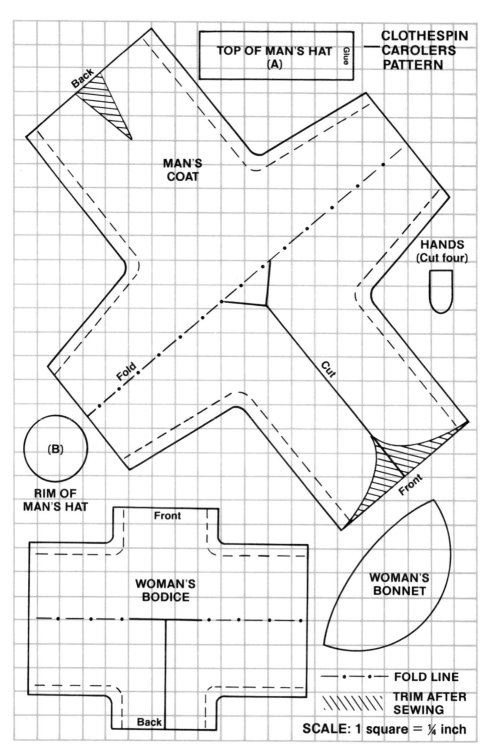

CLOTHESPIN CAROLERS PATTERN

TOP OF MAN'S HAT (A)
Glue

Back

MAN'S COAT

HANDS (Cut four)

Fold

Cut

(B)

RIM OF MAN'S HAT

Front

WOMAN'S BODICE

WOMAN'S BONNET

Back

Front

— • — • — FOLD LINE

\\\\\\\\\ TRIM AFTER SEWING

SCALE: 1 square = ¼ inch

PAPER STARS

Paper is an easy and handy medium to work with, and with wonderful results! What do you have around the house? Use construction paper, metallic foil, gift wrap, drawing paper or whatever else strikes your fancy to make the following ornaments!

You will need:

paper	ruler
pencil	scissors

FIVE - POINTED STAR

Instructions:

1. Fold a square piece of paper in half *diagonally* to make a triangle. (See Diagram 1.)
2. Measure to find the center along side A-D. Bring point B over to this center mark. (See Diagram 2.)
3. Fold corner A upwards so that the crease runs along side B-E. (See Diagram 3.)
4. Fold the right half of the paper behind line A-E as shown in Diagram 4. This part of the paper goes on the outside of what you have been working on . . . not the inside.
5. Turn the shape over to the back and cut along the slanting line shown in Diagram 5. You may have to readjust your folds to make the points line up exactly. Two points of the star will be slightly shorter than the other three. Unfold and enjoy!

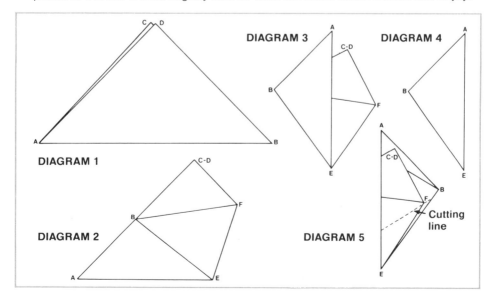

SIX-POINTED STAR

Instructions:

1. Place a square piece of paper in a diamond position and fold it into a triangle, bringing the bottom point to the top point.
2. Fold the triangle into a second triangle by folding it in half as shown in Diagram 1.
3. Fold the triangle into approximate thirds as shown in Diagrams 2 and 3. The center section will be smaller. Side A-E lines up with fold C-E and side D-E lines up with fold B-E.
4. Cut across as shown in Diagram 4. Unfold and enjoy!

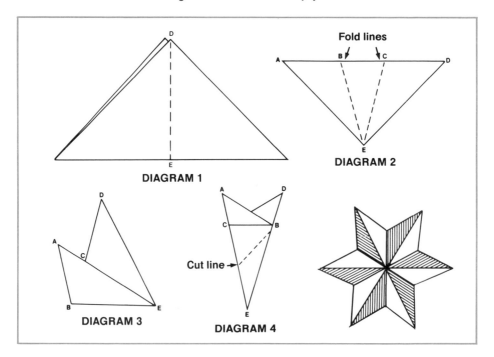

DIAGRAM 1

Fold lines

DIAGRAM 2

DIAGRAM 3

Cut line →

DIAGRAM 4

Note: The six-pointed star can be creased across the points or scored through the points. The center can be cut out and a candle inserted for a Christmasy touch to your table or mantelpiece.

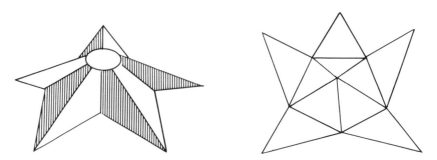

26

STRAW WEAVING

A centuries-old folkcraft, straw has been woven into stars, dolls, butterflies, birds, bells and all sorts of decorative items in all the grain-growing countries of the world. Try crafting a few of these unique ornaments yourself to give a wonderful rustic, traditional touch to your tree. But before you start any of the ornaments on the next two pages, read through the following information on gathering grain, preparing materials and general techniques.

Gathering Grain:

If you live where you can gather your own grain, cut it when it is almost dry—about a week or two before harvesting—and hang in loose bundles with the heads all at one end so it can dry well. If you don't have access to a grain field, you can purchase straw from a floral supply store, feed store or some craft stores. When the straw is dry, clean it by cutting above the first joint and sliding the sheaf away. Cut just below the heads with a razor blade or art knife unless the instructions call for the entire stalk.

Preparing Materials and General Techniques:

When you are ready to use your grain for weaving, soak the cleaned straw in a large pan of very hot water for at least 20 minutes, until the straw bends without splitting or breaking. Wrap the softened straw in a large, wet towel to keep it in a workable condition. (Leftover straw can be dried and stored in large, covered boxes for several months. Mothballs in the boxes will help keep insects and rodents away. Remember that straw resoaked for later use will become darker with each soaking.)

Use a clove hitch knot to tie straw together, below heads when beginning a project, and when plaiting or weaving is completed. Follow this diagram to form knot. Pull thread at both ends to tighten and tie an overhand knot to finish.

When weaving, work approximately two-thirds of the straw length, adding a new straw when necessary. To do this, cut the working straw (the straw being moved into position) at an angle and insert the narrow end of a new straw. Do not add more than one straw at the same place or you will have a weak joint.

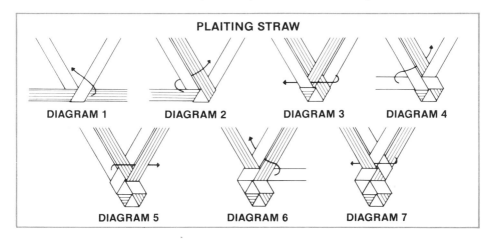

PLAITING STRAW

DIAGRAM 1	DIAGRAM 2	DIAGRAM 3	DIAGRAM 4

DIAGRAM 5	DIAGRAM 6	DIAGRAM 7

STRAW BELL

A symbol of bells that ring in glad Christmas cheer, these straw ornaments can be woven yourself from scratch, or already plaited straw can be purchased at a crafts store.

You will need:

straw (plain or plaited)
bowl of hot water and wet towel
string
scissors
narrow red ribbon

staples and stapler
sprig of holly
sprig of red berries (available from
craft stores)
needle and red thread
red cord or fishing line

Instructions:

Before you begin weaving, read the information on preparing materials and general techniques on page 27.

1. If you are plaiting your own straw, dampen long lengths and braid according to the plaiting diagrams. (See Diagrams 1-7, page 27.) Add new straws as needed at staggered intervals.
2. Make or cut two lengths of straw plait 6" long and two lengths of straw plait 1½" long.
3. Staple the ends of one short length of straw to the ends of one long length of straw as shown in Diagram 8. Fold the second 6" length of straw over this form and staple the other short piece of straw to this as shown in Diagram 9.
4. Staple the bottom short pieces together where they cross in the center of the bell bottom.
5. Sew a sprig of holly to the top of the bell with red thread. Leave enough thread to tie a red ribbon on top of this. Push the wire ends of the artificial berries through the bottom of the bell and secure.
6. Hang with a red cord loop or a loop of fishing line.

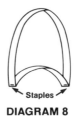

DIAGRAM 8

DIAGRAM 9

BAKER'S CLAY ORNAMENTS

Salt, flour and water . . . mix them together and you're all set to start making easy, inexpensive ornaments that are limited only by your imagination! Here's a project for the whole family to enjoy. Start with this basic recipe and try your hand at this time-honored craft.

You will need:

4 cups all-purpose flour
1 cup salt
1½ cups water
acrylic paints
polyurethane varnish

Instructions:

1. Mix the salt and flour together. Add water and stir.
2. Turn the mixture out on a floured surface and knead like bread until the dough obtains a smooth, putty-like consistency. This will take about 10 minutes.
3. Wrap the Baker's Clay tightly in plastic to keep it from drying out. It can be stored in the refrigerator, but you should use it up within a few days of mixing.

Baker's Clay is similar to regular clay. By pinching, poking, rolling, coiling, forming slabs and cutting you can design your own ornaments. Try cutting out shapes with your favorite Christmas cookie cutters, but be sure not to make the ornaments too large or they will weight down the branches of your tree. Before you bake your creations (one to two hours at 350° F.), insert a wire from a paper clip for a hanger. After baking, cool and paint with acrylics, then spray with polyurethane varnish.
Here are two irresistible designs for you to try using walnut shells.

BUG SLEIGH

Here's a funny little fellow to add to your tree for some extra Christmas cheer.

You will need:

Baker's Clay (see above)
1 half walnut shell
2 straight pins
floral wire
paper clip and scissors
glaze made by adding 2 tablespoons instant coffee to 1 beaten egg
acrylic paints and paintbrush
polyurethane varnish (available from craft stores)

Instructions:

1. Roll a large Baker's Clay ball and place it in the walnut shell to form the bug's body.
2. Roll a smaller ball for the head. Place it on top of the larger ball, using a small dab of water to join the two together.
3. Insert the straight pins into the head for antennae. (See Diagram 1.)
4. Insert the floral wire on each side of the body for arms and bend into the desired position. Make Baker's Clay balls for hands and stick them on the ends of the floral wire as shown in Diagram 2.
5. Roll tubes of clay for sleigh runners and sit the shell on top of them as shown in Diagram 3.

6. Roll a long, thin strip for the scarf and carefully wrap it in place around the bug's neck.
7. Clip off a piece of the paper clip and bend it into a hanger wire. Insert it into the bug's back.
8. Place the ornament on a cookie sheet and bake for one to two hours at 350° F.
9. Glaze while still hot with the egg and coffee glaze. Paint on details with acrylics when cool; varnish when dry.

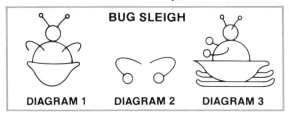

BUG SLEIGH

DIAGRAM 1   DIAGRAM 2   DIAGRAM 3

NURSERY MOUSE

This sweet little sleeper is easy and fun to make!

You will need:

Baker's Clay (see recipe on page 29)
one half walnut shell
floral wire
glaze made by adding 2 tablespoons instant coffee to 1 beaten egg
acrylic paints and paintbrush

polyurethane varnish (available from craft stores)
piece of eyelet or lacy trim 3" long and 1½" wide
thin ribbon 20" long
liquid white glue

Instructions:

1. Roll a ball of Baker's Clay (A) and place it in the walnut shell for the body. (See Diagram 1.) Be sure to fill the shell.
2. Roll out a small strip for the blanket fold (B); place it on top of the body using a small dab of water to join. (See Diagram 1.)
3. Roll a mouse-shaped head. Attach ears with a dab of water; attach the head to the body with a dab of water. Add a tiny ball nose. (See Diagram 2.)
4. Make little Baker's Clay paws (C). Place them on top of the blanket fold with a dab of water. (See Diagram 3.)
5. Insert a floral wire hoop into the clay towards the back for a canopy. (See Diagram 3.)
6. Prop the ornament on a cookie sheet with foil supports or position it in the oven rack so it is secure. Bake at 350° F. for one to two hours, until it is hard.
7. Glaze while hot. Paint when cool with acrylics. Paint the floral wire hoop white. Varnish when dry.
8. Gather the eyelet or trim on one side to form the canopy. (See Diagram 4.) Check for size fit on hoop before tying off gathers.
9. Wrap the ribbon around the bottom of the shell and weave it through the holes in the eyelet canopy front. Tie in a bow at the top and leave long ends of ribbon for hanging. (See Diagram 5.)
10. Glue the canopy and ribbon to the floral wire hoop and the bottom of the shell to secure.

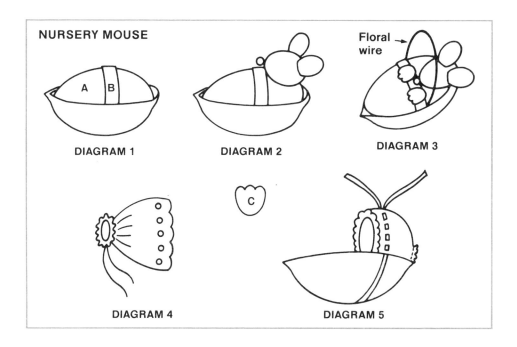

NURSERY MOUSE

DIAGRAM 1

DIAGRAM 2

Floral wire

DIAGRAM 3

DIAGRAM 4

DIAGRAM 5

WALNUT ORNAMENTS

Have a bunch of leftover walnut shells? Here are a couple of quick and easy ornaments to make that are as clever as they are simple!

WALNUT STRAWBERRY

You will need:

2 walnut halves
liquid white glue
acrylic paints and paintbrush
yellow seed beads (optional)

green felt
scissors
needle and thread
gold cord

Instructions:

1. Glue the two halves together.
2. Paint the walnut shell bright red. When dry, paint on yellow spots or glue on yellow seed beads.
3. Cut a "crown" of leaves from the felt. Sew gold cord through the top of the crown and tie in a loop for hanging.
4. Glue the leaves and cord to the top of the strawberry.

WALNUT MOUSE

You will need:

1 walnut half
small piece of cardboard or heavy paper
liquid white glue

scraps of fabric and gray and red felt
2 black seed beads
brown embroidery floss
scissors

Instructions:

1. Place the shell on top of the cardboard; trace around the shell. Cut out around tracing and glue cardboard as bottom to the shell.
2. Cut out a 3" diameter circle from the fabric scrap. Sew a running stitch around the edge of the fabric and gather. Glue in place on top of the walnut shell to make a cap. (See Diagram 1.)
3. Cut out gray felt ears; glue them in place on the cap (A). Glue two small circles for decoration between the ears (B). (See Diagram 2.)
4. Glue the seed beads in place for eyes (C).
5. Cut three 2" lengths of embroidery floss. Tie them together in the middle and glue below eyes for whiskers (D).
6. Glue a long piece of embroidery floss to the back for a tail (E). Cut a bow-shaped piece of red felt and glue to the end of the tail (F).
7. Stitch a thread (G) through the top of the cap and tie in a loop for hanging.

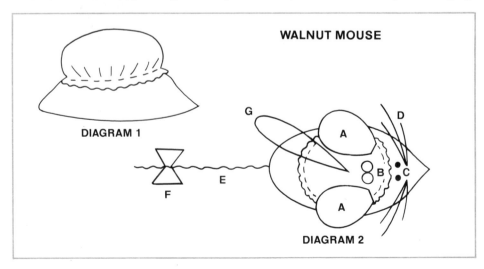

WALNUT MOUSE

DIAGRAM 1

DIAGRAM 2